THE UNHEARD VOICES OF MUNDHWA

STORIES OF ENDURANCE AND SURVIVAL

EMPATHETIC HUMANS

Dedicated to iTeach RSM School, Mundhwa, Pune for always supporting unconventional ideas and encouraging us to push our limits.

Contents

Contents

Preface

Pune is a land of dreams for everyone. People believe that Pune is one of the platforms where they can set themselves up. A progressive city in Maharashtra. But the same Pune also has another side that we look at every day but don't understand and this is the aspect of poverty. The world around us is rapidly evolving but there are some individuals who are not able to move even one single step.

On one hand, we strongly say that don't judge a book by its cover but on the other hand, we are discriminating between people based on their living. We shouldn't ignore the people in bad conditions. We always learn good things like we should help and support everyone, but where few implement it. We say that we help people, but if we would have helped, then in our country, poverty should have been a thing of the past. If every person would have helped just another person who needs help, then in our country poverty should have disappeared.

When we say struggle then our mind just thinks about successful people who have come out of their struggles. But there are also many people who are struggling in poverty but they don't get that one chance to prove themselves. All of us would have seen various companies and people come from different places to work in it. But the people who are living next to us are struggling even for that one meal.

You would get to read multiple such revelations in this book through those stories but we want you to put yourself in their place and think about how you would feel.

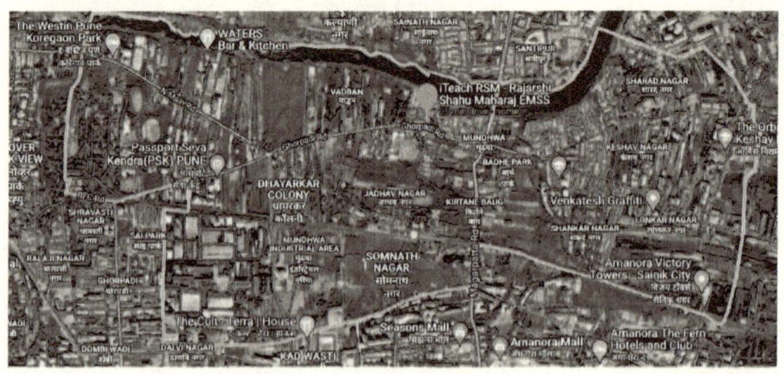

Map of Mundhwa, Pune

Mundhwa is a small place in Pune where all these stories belong. We have tried to show these unseen & unheard sides of Pune. The unheard voices come to us every day but no one really hears them. Everyone ignores it and thinks- Why should we help? or How could we help? We don't even realize that if we help someone who really needs it then that person will always keep in mind that, "Yes, there are people who also listen to us."

These are the voices of those Unheard Humans. All the stories start the same way but go on different trajectories, just like LIFE!

How we wrote

We all were very nervous before taking the interviews but once we heard them out, it was liberating as well as shocking. Liberating, due to the courage showed by us and shocking because of the magnitude of struggles in their life. After reading a few stories, you might feel how easily they are talking with us. This definitely does not look real. But this was not our first interview. We got rejected by multiple people and then finally we got an interview that was worth sharing.

Also, a few of the protagonists didn't give consent to sharing their personal details in the book so we removed their selfies and replaced their names with their first initials, whereas the remaining of them gave us consent, so we used their selfies, but to maintain the consistency in the book, their name is also replaced with their initial letter.

Lastly, a few similarly themed stories have been collated to give a stronger impact but most of them are by individual co-author.

About Us

Empathetic Humans is a code name for the Grade 9 Class Students of the year 2021-22 of iTeach RSM School, Mundwa, Pune. It is a Public-Private-Partnership English Medium school that intakes all the government school students after 7th grade and provides free & excellent education. We live near the Mundhwa area and we have completed this phenomenal feat of creating this book by going out there on the streets of Mundhwa and voicing out those unheard voices in this book.

Contact Us

We would love to connect with you and hear your thoughts, feedback, and actions that we together could take to address the social problems.

Shoot us an email at: *empathetichumans@gmail.com*

-**Empathetic Humans (*July 2022*)**

Acknowledgements

This book is inspired by the book 'Fatal Accidents of Birth' by **Harsh Mander**. This book is the result of overcoming our comfort zone, pushing our limits, and going out on the streets to interact with humans who have been deprived of any privileges for far too long. Below are the courageous and empathetic souls who brought out these stories:

Unseen co-authors of this book!

1. Aaniya Shaikh
2. Aarti Sharma
3. Aashitosh Gaud
4. Akash Deokar
5. Amit Sharma
6. Anuj Jadhav
7. Anushka T. Mishra
8. Aryan Gaikwad
9. Ashpak Ladaf
10. Buddha Jyoti Gautam
11. Dyaneshwari Gaikwad
12. Ganesh Kumbhar

13. Gun Jadhav
14. Kanchan Kol
15. Khushi Salunke
16. Krishna Sadigale
17. Kundan Verma
18. Mayuresh Kamble
19. Nandini Giri
20. Naziya Shaikh
21. Neha Pawar
22. Nitesh Yadav
23. Pooja Bodekar
24. Pooja Gupta
25. Prachi Wade
26. Prajakta Gaud
27. Praniti Kapure
28. Pushpa Ram
29. Rachana Mali
30. Rohan Shinde
31. Samruddhi More
32. Saurabh Verma
33. Shraddha Singh
34. Shweta Gaud
35. Suhani Dwivedi
36. Sumit Nath
37. Tanishka Jadhav
38. Tejaswee Hole
39. Vedant Pawar
40. Vidhi Bagade
41. Vidya Tate
42. Vishal Kumbhar
43. Vishvajeet Patil
44. Vrushabh Gawade
45. Yana Gumle

This book wouldn't have been possible without the initial brainstorming with **Ms. Suchita Mohan** and **Ms. Mohini Pandey**. Also, every member of **iTeach RSM staff** has been really supportive and appreciative of our work which pushed us to take this project to the final destination.

The ground research and the corresponding story have been written by the above co-authors but to make it more presentable, 4 young humans among them have edited and enhanced these stories. These 4 young editors are **Pooja Gupta, Rachana Mali, Nitesh Yadav,** and **Shraddha Singh**.

Special thanks to **Ms. Azeema Chimthanawala** for patiently editing & reviewing the book. She incorporated her holistic thoughts in this book and was always ready to brainstorm about the enhancement of the structure and how to pitch the book to the world.

Huge thanks to **Ms. Neha Vaidya, Ms. Meera Krishnan, Ms. Namita Agarwal, and Ms. Suchita Mohan** for reviewing the manuscript and gifting us with their valuable perspective and suggestions.

Lastly but most importantly, this book is incomplete without one human and that is our Role model, Guide, Motivator, Mentor, and English teacher- **Mr. Aman Gupta,** who guided us through the process of taking the Interviews and translating them into coherent stories. He introduced us to the book 'Fatal Accident of Birth' by Harsh Mander and helped us to dive deep into it. He was the first person who noticed these unheard voices and invested us in the idea of writing this book as a part of our English Project.

He not only teaches us English but also plays a very important role in developing us as empathetic humans. He didn't just help us to write this book but also taught us multiple skills like Public speaking, Standup Comedy, Blogging, Active listening, etc, which have always thrown us out of our comfort zone and brought us growth in life. One quote which he keeps reiterating in the class is *'Life becomes more beautiful when we get out of our comfort zone'*, which has always motivated us. He always strives to make us unique with his mind-blowing thoughts and ideas. He doesn't just give space to make our ideas real but also takes equal efforts to make them possible. **We can proudly say that he is the best potter of our life, who has given a perfect and beautiful shape to our shapeless minds.**

-Empathetic Humans (*July 2022*)

Part 1: Introduction

CHAPTER ONE

WHAT AND WHY, BOTH ARE IMPORTANT

-**Interviewed By** Kundan Verma, Anuj Jadhav, Vidya Tate
& Krishna Sadigale
-**Collated By** Rachana Mali

Whenever we do something, there is always a reason behind it. Is it necessary that both What and Why must be right? Many times, actions can be wrong but why that action was taken might be justifiable. We always see the action done by people but have we ever tried to figure out, why they did that action? What's the compulsion which is forcing humans to do that? Below are a few short life stories that elaborate on this thought.

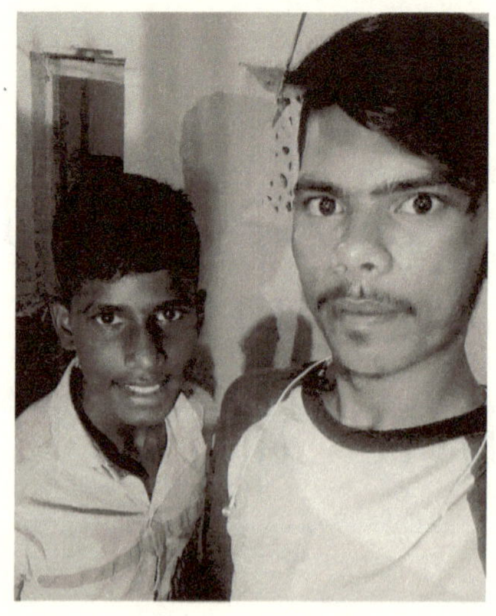

Interaction with Mr. D

Once Kundan and Anuj met a Panipuri seller and they took his interview. His name was Mr. D. He was not with his dad since a young age. Therefore he was not educated but he was good at cooking. As he did not have much money to invest, he decided to open one small Panipuri stall. He started selling Panipuri as a roadside vendor. Whenever Police came around and saw these stalls on the footpath, they confiscated their stalls saying, "It's illegal to set up your business on the footpath". And when the Police confiscated their stalls, it took around 2-3 days to release them. He would sleep hungry on those days hoping to get back to his stall. Anuj felt guilty after listening to this as he doesn't complete his lunch or dinner and throws the remaining. Later, Anuj asked, "What help do you want from the government?" He replied,

"The only thing I want is solace. People like me already don't have money to survive. In such difficult situations also we try to be self-reliant and start something by ourselves but the government doesn't allow us to do so!"

Interaction with Ms. R

Vidya met a lady whose name was Ms. R. She sells flowers on the Mundhwa signal. Every day she needed to work hard for food. She wanted to study and change her situation. It was her dream to pull her family out of poverty but she didn't get admission to any of the schools because she did not have any of the documents. The unavailability of the documents broke her dream into small-small pieces. Later Vidya asked her, "What help do you want from the government?" Then she replied,

"I understand that it's very important to have an identity document, but I don't think identity is important for students. If schools had given me a chance to study in school without the documents, then I might have been able to create my identity today."

Interaction with Mr. B

Krishna had met one person on a Mundhwa signal as well. His name was Mr. B. He was handicapped and was begging over there. Krishna decided to interview him. He was an orphan from a young age. He didn't remember his childhood, but all he remembered was that he used to beg. He didn't remember the location because every time he needed to change it. When someone saw beggars begging on the street, they informed the Police, and without thinking the Police just hit them with batons because it's not allowed to beg in Pune. Krishna could sense the pain in his voice. Later, Krishna asked him what he wanted to tell society, and he replied,

> *"I am handicapped since birth. There is not a single place where I can get a job nor am I allowed to beg. Life has become a curse for me."*

Making rules is important but while making them we should also see all sides because not always every side is the same. There are some rules which are unfair in our society. According to one side maybe it's fitting perfectly but there are some innocent people whose lives are becoming more difficult because of some of these rules.

When we say they should have an identity document, we are forgetting to see why they don't have it. When we tell them that they are not allowed to set up their business on the footpath, we are forgetting to acknowledge where they can set up and how they can bring food on their plates and feed their family.

If you are reading this book, most probably you are one among the privileged ones for whom having an identity document or having food on their plate is very basic and you might take it for granted. But for some, it is a challenge that threatens their very living.

CHAPTER TWO

UNSTABLE SEESAW

-Interviewed By Samruddhi More & Neha Pawar
-Collated By Rachana Mali

What does development mean? Is it just about building lots of industries, lots of buildings, and growth in technology?

According to me, development means much more. Building humanity, establishing fair rules, and making a safe society are also part of development. Whenever we play the game of Seesaw, we always need to maintain balance. If we need to maintain balance in small games then don't you think the same applies to society?

While maintaining balance in a Seesaw, it's not just about how much we weigh down, but it also depends on the weight of our partner on the opposite side. But in real life, people are just focused on personal development, and not many care for others and this is where we are losing the balance. We have spoken with some people in our society and the following are 2 of the many stories that came our way.

Samruddhi was walking on the footpath in search of homeless humans when she met a lady who was begging.

She spoke with that lady and she got to know her name was Ms. D. She was from Pune itself. As she had lost both of her parents at a young age, she was raised by her Uncle and Aunt. They married her off at the age of 14 years only. Later she gave birth to a baby girl but her in-laws were very disappointed because they were expecting a boy. So one day when D was sleeping, her husband killed her little princess. In fear, she ran away and started begging on Mundhwa's signal.

Interaction with Ms. S

Neha had met a Housemaid. Her name was Ms. S. Since childhood, she belonged to a poor family. Her father passed away when she was 8 years old. From a young age, struggles had chosen her. She started working as a maid when she was just 8 years old. She got married at the age of 19. Her in-laws ' conditions were also not good, so she needed to continue working as a Housemaid. Later Neha asked her what help she wanted from society or the government. She replied that from a young age, she has seen her mother working as a maid, but she never saw her getting respect anywhere. She continued,

> "*Working as a maid is our compulsion, but people are making it our weakness. Whenever I enter any of the houses, people always tell me Chori ki to seeda Police station le jaungi (If you steal something then we will directly take you to the Police Station). Everyone believes that maids are thieves, just because we are poor.*"

Both of these stories make me think, is Pune a developed city? People are struggling for basic rights of equality and respect. If this society has not given equal rights to females as of now, by when people of the LGBTQ+ community would get their equal rights? If this society has not given respect to housemaids as of now, by when people would give respect to sanitation workers? In the 21st century also people are not able to understand- What is true gender equality? What is it like to give equal respect to fellow humans? Then will it be?

Part 2: Identity Crisis

CHAPTER THREE

WHAT IS OUR IDENTITY?

-By Gun Jadhav

Interaction with Ms. R

I remember that on my way back home, I see a lot of humans sitting on the footpath. I have always ignored them and never really cared to talk with them. As my friends and I mostly think and talk about the people who have higher social status than us and not them.

This time it was different, I had a notebook in my hand with all the interview questions, which I had jotted down to ask these homeless humans. For the first time, I noticed them carefully and approached one of the ladies who was busy making a flower garland. I asked her, "What is your name, Didi?" She replied to me that her name was Ms. R.

On further conversation, she started sharing with me about her childhood. She shared that from a young age, she belonged to a poor family. Her father used to work on a construction site. They used to get very little money and therefore she was not able to go to school. And at the age of 20, she got married. Her husband used to make flower garlands for survival. She also joined the same job. Later, she gave birth to two children.

Even though her in-laws' house condition was not good, she still fought with her husband for sending their children to school, as she knew how hard life is without education. She wanted to make her children educated and after lots of arguments, her in-laws agreed to send her children to school. When she went to a government school for admission, they were asked for documents. But they did not have any documents. She requested the principal, she begged them but no one showed sympathy to her.

Her financial condition was so bad that if she didn't work for a single day, she would not be able to put food on the table for her family. So she gave up and now even her children are working to survive at a very young age.

At this point, I thought of suggesting Ms. R try admission to my school but soon I realized that it starts from 8th grade and is not applicable for her children. Later I asked her if she wanted anything from the government. She replied,

"I just want the government to support my children's education. I believe that a child without education is a building without a foundation."

After listening to her, I felt very depressed. I never thought that people go through so many struggles every single day for food. Also, I was unable to comprehend that **"How could one sheet of paper represent a person's identity?"**

CHAPTER FOUR

My Life Looks Like Hell

-By Khushi Salunke

Interaction with Ms. A

Once we got our Project to interview unprivileged humans in our community, I actively started to observe all the humans on the footpath. Usually, on my way to school, I see a woman living on a footpath. I observed her for 2-3 days and finally decided to speak with her. I requested her for some time and started interacting with her.

Her name was Ms. A. She was from Solapur and her age was 22. She belonged to a poor family. When she was

8 years old, her father died in an accident. Suddenly her world changed. She wanted to study and become self-reliant. But after her father's death, her mother was not able to send her to school. She left her school when she was 8 years old and started working for the survival of the family along with her mother.

She got married at the age of 15. Her husband was the victim of alcoholism. Therefore, they were facing lots of economic instability and because of it, they had to leave their house. They came on footpaths with their two children.

She wanted her children to study and be someone in their life, but they did not have any kind of documents. Therefore she failed to put her children in school. She takes her children to sell flowers with her on the signal. Ms. A and her children used to work very hard to sell their flowers, but still, no one used to buy flowers from them. They were suffering from a very hard time. Sometimes her children don't get any food to eat for two days, so they are forced to beg. She said, "If the Police see us, they would abuse us and it felt very insulting."

Lately, they are able to earn enough money for food. But at night time, her husband comes in a drunken state and takes all the money away from her. She also tried to complain at the Police Station but every time Police used to disrespect her, refusing to register her complaint. At last, she said,

> *"Har din sooraj ki kirne nayi samasya leke aati hain, zindagi hamari nark se bhi battar hain(Each day the sun rises with problems. Sometimes I feel that my life is worse than hell)."*

It was very shocking to hear her story. I realized that family support is so crucial for child growth. Without them, childhood just vanishes as it happened with Ms. A. Also, I realized that it's so difficult to live a life with dignity without identity documents. We are just losing the human potential by not helping these people and until we include them in our mainstream economy, **I don't think India can ever become a superpower.**

Part 3: The Survival

CHAPTER FIVE

Same Day, Different Stories

-By Shweta Gaud

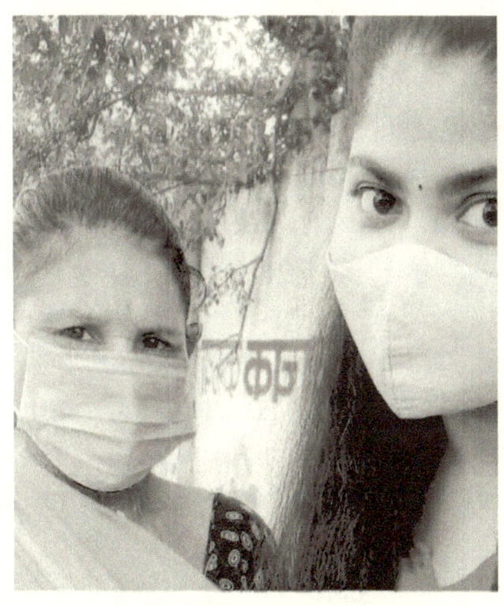

Interaction with Ms. S

That day, I remember it was cold. I was shivering. I didn't want to go to school, but I came out of my blanket as my mom started calling me. As usual, I got ready and went to school. The day was very tiring but my tiffin made me happy. When school got over, I took my earphones from my bag, played music, and started walking home.

Suddenly I saw a woman on the side of the road with a man beside her. He was sleeping on a footpath. The woman had dirty torn clothes on her. Everything was surrounded by her belongings which included some clothes, blankets, and some toys. I was wondering, in the morning if I could not step out of my blanket, how could this woman who has nothing to cover herself, feel?

I wasn't able to stop myself, I went to her and I was like, "Hello, aunty". She looked at me and she must be thinking, "Why is she here?". I explained to her that I wanted to interview her for my school project and she thankfully agreed. I asked her name, and she replied, "Ms. S". I asked her, "Why are you here on the footpath?" the way she looked at me with those wet eyes, just broke my heart.

Ms. S was a 30-year-old lady with her husband living on the footpath. Her living room, her kitchen, her bedroom everything was confined to that footpath. Her husband was ill. She told me her husband was an alcoholic with a damaged liver. Now he is not able to move, he just keeps lying on the floor. The government helped with her husband's treatment by giving him medicines and keeping him in a government hospital for 15 days, but it was of no use.

She further said that when it rains, she barely finds a space to go and sit because she doesn't have any shelter. She sells kid toys or begs on the road for a living. She added, "Why would people buy something from the road for their kids? People rarely take it from me. I beg I eat." I got emotional after hearing this.

She has two kids. They are in boarding school and she goes to meet them once every 3 months. She does not have anyone else in the family. Her mom and dad died when she was just a kid. She got married and her father-in-law and mother-in-law also died soon after. She was alone with her two kids and ill husband. Her kids are in one boarding school, they are just 5 and 6 years old. She could not keep them with her, they are safe and studying. She does not want them to face these situations which she is facing right now. "It is really hard! But this is life", she said.

> "*I have realised that life is hard but you have to walk, accept situations, tackle them, stand up strong and face them with a big smile. And nothing is permanent, everything keeps changing, good times are yet to come.*"

Heart touching, right! These are not my words, this is what Ms. S said and taught me an important life lesson.

I felt helpless and found it difficult to understand the amount of pain that Ms. S has gone through. I understand that the morning sun is the same for everyone but the story of every single human varies. Some people are happy in their homes, laughing and eating whereas some people are on the roads, struggling and begging for food.

THRASHED TO TRASH

-By Rohan Shinde

I remember, one day I was going back home and I saw a man searching for something in the trash. I felt that I should help him, so I went to him and asked, "Uncle, What are you searching for, can I help you?" He got scared and put all the plastic out of his bag and started saying, "Sorry-Sorry". I consoled him, gave him some water, and asked him what was the matter?

I didn't intend to take his interview as such but saw an opportunity here. So I asked him to tell his whole story. First, he told me that his name is Mr. S. He came to Pune in search of a job with his wife and two sons. Initially, he used to live near Pune station but later he got to know that he will get more money in Mundhwa, so he shifted to Mundhwa and started working here.

In 2020, the woeful tragedy of Covid attacked the whole country. It also demolished him. Because of Lockdown, he lost his job. It was very hard for him to just bring food for his family. His house owner also pulled him out because he didn't pay rent for 5 months.

It was very hard to get another home without money. It was also impossible to get another job during a pandemic. They lived on the footpath for two days. He said, "It was very hard for me to see my son suffer at a younger age."

He decided to leave both his kids at the orphanage house and started living on a footpath and begging with his wife. People passing from the footpath didn't give him respect at all. They both used to starve for two-three days. So he started collecting plastic from trash and started selling it at a shop.

After he finished sharing his struggles, he started saying, "I was not spreading trash, I was just collecting it, so that we can get some money for food."

It was sad to hear his story. I was feeling very helpless. I gave him some food and asked, "What help do you want from the government?". He said,

"I just want one safe house so that I can bring my kids back and give them a safe and secure future."

After listening to him I got to know how hard our parents need to work for us. I get upset if my parents say that they can't give me chocolate or my favorite gadget whereas some children need to live away from their parents.

CHAPTER SEVEN

STIGMAS OF SOCIETY

-By Rachana Mali

Interaction with Ms. H

Once I was walking down the street. And because of the rainfall, I decided to wait at the bus stop for a while. Next to the bus stop, I saw one family sitting under a hut, which was in very bad condition. They were eating food over there. Behind that footpath, there was lots of trash. Lots of mosquitoes were there and sewage water was overflowing. It was a really cold atmosphere and their children were sitting naked.

In some time, one car passed through the street and they splashed all the muddy water on them. The people at the bus stop shouted at the driver but that family was quiet. It was a very helpless moment for me. Anyways, I went to my house. I saw them again the next day and decided to interact with them for my English Project.

Once the aunty finished with her food, I asked her for some time and we started a conversation. She first told me her name- Ms. H. She continued that she was from Nepal. In her childhood, there was a lack of hospitals in her village. Her father used to tell her that because of the lack of hospitals, they decided to give her birth in the house itself. Unfortunately, it was cesarean delivery. Ironically, the happiest moment of her birth came with the grief of her mother's death. My soul shook after listening to this.

Because of that incident, most of her relatives used to call her the "**Stigma of the house**". And at one point, she also started feeling shame for herself. Due to these feelings, she left her school in 3rd standard, and at age of 17, she got married to a 19-year-old boy named Pandu Pawar. Similar to Ms. H, her husband also did not have a mother.

Exactly after one year of her marriage, her father-in-law passed away due to a heart attack. At her in-law's house, she used to face taunting and disgrace from the other family members. Due to continuous quarrels, Pandu's elder brother asked them to leave their house.

At the same time, Ms. H was 4 months pregnant. So she and her husband decided to go to some city where they can give a good atmosphere to their future child, so they decided to come to Pune.

When they came to Pune, they stayed at the railway station for the first night but on another day, they roamed around in search of a job. After lots of effort, her husband found a housekeeping job in one fast-food hotel. They also found a small iron sheet house, the same day. Her husband used to get only 2 to 3 thousand rupees per month from which they were only able to give rent, so she also started working as a housemaid. Everything was going well.

Later, they gave birth to a beautiful little prince who they named Sarthak. When Sarthak was two years old in 2019, the black clouds of the pandemic came on them.

Not just on them, but it was the worst year for the whole world. A virus named Covid-19 was spreading everywhere and because the whole world was in lockdown, no one was allowed to step out of their house.

Because of this Covid-19, unfortunately, that resort where her husband was working shut down forever. For one-two months they had groceries to survive but after two months everything was over. There was no food to eat, no job to do and outside there was a dark pandemic. Later she said for some time, they were feeling *Maut ne to checkmate diya hain, ghar mein rahenge to bhook se mar jayenge aur bahar jayenge to corona se* (It seems like Death has given us a checkmate. If we stay at home then we will die due to hunger and if we step out then due to corona).

But for their child, her husband courageously stepped out in search of a job. He did not get any job but policemen beat him badly with their batons. The next day both of them were sitting disappointed.

Till then, their house owner came and pulled them out of their house. It was very sad for them. They were completely hopeless. There was no way for them. Later she said *Jee to sakte the nahi, par sukun se mar bhi nahi sakte the, hath mein ek baccha jo tha* (We didn't feel like living anymore, but can't peacefully die also because we were having a kid in our hands).

So looking at the child they stayed on the footpath, putting one plastic sheet as the roof of their child. It was the same roof they are sitting on now. It has been around 2 years since that incident and they are still in the same condition.

Later I asked her, "Why don't you ask something from the Government?" Then she replied that the government wants proof of poverty and as she is from Nepal, she doesn't even have a Ration card. In India, if you have a blue, pink, or yellow Ration card, then you can get a subsidized rate on food grains. She continued,

> "*Ironically, if the person in good condition has a yellow color Ration card, then they are considered below poverty line, but those who don't have a Ration card are invisible to government. Actually it's not their fault, it's all because of me as I am born with **stigma** for my family.*"

After listening to her story it was understandable that at every point of her life a problem is waiting to trouble her. There is not a single page in her life book where she was satisfied with her life. I was confused that how can people deal with such difficult life? I have so many things but still, I am full of excuses whereas she was quiet as nighttime.

It is very sad that in the 21st century, even after 74 years of independence, people believe these stigmas and superstitions. Not only do they believe it but they are also pulling others downwards because of that mindset.

CHAPTER EIGHT

TIME IS IRREVERSIBLE

-By Pooja Bodekar

I remember on my way back home, I had eaten Pani-Puri from one of the Uncle's stalls multiple times. I observe him every day and whenever I see him, he used to look in tension. If some people come to buy Pani-Puri, at that moment only, he used to talk with those people. Otherwise, he looked sad. So, I decided to ask him about his life, but I was feeling uncomfortable approaching him. Still, I tried to speak with him, and I went to his shop. I requested him to make a video about him and his family. He was quiet for a minute, then after some time he said: "Yes, you can take my video."

His name was Mr. R. He had a small stall to sell Pani-Puri. When he was a child, he did not go to school because he thought that after studying also, they do the same job only. For him, school was a boring thing. When his parents told him to go to school and do his studies, he never listened to them, and just ignored them. When he started growing up, he got to know the value of studies and he is feeling regret, that now, no one is there to shout at him for studies.

At the age of 18, he got married. Now he has three children and his children go to the government school. If his children ask for something, he doesn't have enough money to buy those things, so he always ignores those requests. His wife also goes to work and earns 2000 rupees per month. So when she gets her payment, she uses it for her children. Uncle R earns 3000 to 4000 rupees per month. He gives it to the room owner because he lives in a rented home and the rent of that home is 5000 rupees per month.

His expectations from the government are that they should give them a home and give admission to their children in a good school. But they are just wild dreams. Now, he regrets that,

> "*If I had listened to my parents, then I would not be in this situation. I would have got a better paying job and my children would also be going to a good school.*"

I felt bad that he is unable to fulfill his wishes and learned that there is an age to do things. And we should listen to our elders and respect what they are saying because our elders never think ill about us. It reminded me of one of the quotes, which states "**ONCE THE TIME IS GONE, IT NEVER COMES BACK.**"

CHAPTER NINE

The Struggles and Growth of a Man

-By Yana Gumle

Interaction with Mr. G

When I was walking to the shop, I saw him. I saw him at the footpath near the Mundhwa signal. His innocence made me want to go and talk to him for my English Project.

He was Mr. G from Pandharpur. He sells handmade flower garlands for 20 rupees per piece. He sells according to the festivals of different seasons.

He was born in a poor family and his father worked very hard after his birth. His father did many things for his future and they were living happily. After his marriage at the age of 16, his father unfortunately died. His family was getting weak and they were not having any work to do. None of his relatives helped him, but his wife supported him a lot and said, "Let's shift to Pune and do some work over there." They both started to sell handmade things.

He didn't have a home. He was staying on a footpath with his children and wife. He has two sons, the younger one is 2 years old and the older one is 7 years old. He buys flowers in the winter for 1000 to 1500 rupees and sells them in the form of garlands to customers. He earns a profit of 600 to 700 rupees in a week and that is sufficient money to fulfill their food needs. But he is still struggling to get a house.

10 years have passed since their marriage and his aim is to make his wife realize that she didn't make a mistake by marrying him and that she should feel that the man she chose was the best decision of her life. She should not be regretting it as from their teenage till now he hasn't given her the things or the life which she wanted. He also wanted to make his children educated so that in the future the struggle he is facing does not get repeated to his children.

When I asked about the Government support he wants. He replied,

*"We want whatever support Government can give,
but no support has reached us till now."*

I felt so proud of him after looking at his spirit and the number of efforts he makes for his family on a daily basis. I got to know that he always thinks about his family rather than himself which made me think about others' feelings before mine.

CHAPTER TEN

THE BROKEN HEART OF WOMEN

-By Ashpak Ladaf

Pune is a city where people come from many different places. Pune is a platform for everyone to explore their dreams. With all the development, there is some poverty as well. Whenever we say Pune, we only think about the development but I got an opportunity to take an interview with an underprivileged person for my English Project to understand the poverty aspect as well.

One fine day I was walking home as usual, but because of heavy rainfall, I was forced to wait. I stood at the bus stop. A woman was sitting next to me. She was freezing because of the cold. Later I requested the same woman for an interview. I asked her, "Could I speak with you for 10 minutes?" She hesitantly agreed.

I asked her about her childhood. After listening to the term "**childhood**", one small smile came on her face. She said that her childhood was the happiest part of her life. She used to go to the farm with her father. Only her brother used to go to school as they did not have enough money to educate both of them.

At the age of 15, she got married to a widowed man who had one son. She was not happy with her match, but because of her parents, she got married to that person. Her husband used to abuse her. So one day she came to her parent's house and said that she wanted a divorce. Her parents refused. They said, "If you get divorced, what will people think about you?" She sadly returned to her in-laws' house and continued to suffer due to the same behavior from her husband. Later, she had two daughters and one son.

As her children were growing. They used to stand against their father for abusing their mother but she used to shout at her children saying, "However he is, he is your father."

One day her husband came home in a drunken state and hit her very badly. As her husband's behavior was beyond the children's capacity to handle, her son called the Police, and they arrested her husband. But as she cared for her husband, she immediately paid the bail for her husband. After her husband came out of jail, he threw her and her children out of their very own house. Now, she is working as a housemaid to survive and feed her children.

Later I asked her if she wanted any help from the government. She replied,

"I just want the government to work on girl's safety. We should take some steps against violence. It's

very important to stand against violence because girls like me always forgive our partner out of love, care and all. But wrong is wrong and we should stand against it."

While reading about domestic violence in our Social Studies class, I always thought that it is a thing of the past but her story changed my perspective. It is still quite prevalent and we should together empower our women to raise voices against this, as the laws are already in place to support them. Also, I realized how important it is to become financially independent, as we never know when our "**close ones**" might turn on us.

CHAPTER ELEVEN

DEPRIVED OF OPPORTUNITIES

-By Aarti Sharma

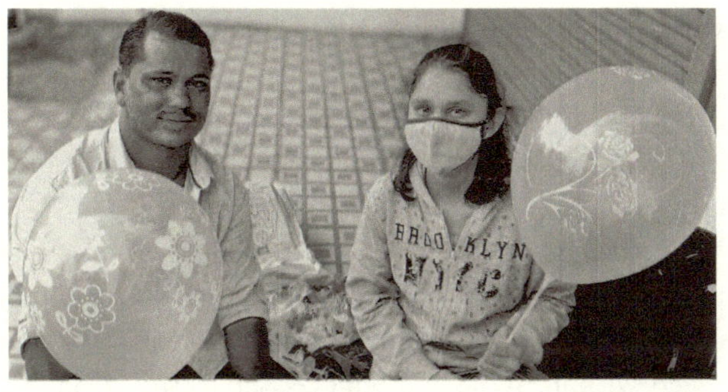

Interaction with Mr. N

I remember that while I was going home after school, I met him. He was from Pune. I talked with him, he was very kind-hearted and he was also giving me respect. His name was Mr. N and he was a balloon seller who was looking exhausted and his clothes were ragged. He was sitting on the footpath and I requested him to share his life journey with me for my English Project.

His childhood was equally challenging as he was from a poor family and at that time, he didn't realize the value of studies. Also, his parents were not able to afford his school fees, so when he got 16 years old, he started selling balloons and garbage bags for money. He worked for their family needs like monthly groceries, clothes, etc. When he reached adulthood his parents married him and the couple gave birth to a daughter. They decided to give the best life and education to their only child.

With years of effort, his daughter successfully graduated from a Christian school. After passing 12th grade, she went to different offices to ask for a job, but the interviewer kept making excuses that she didn't have all the documents. The interviewers have just been avoiding her for six years, and now they have lost all hopes and she is jobless helping with her own household chores.

Their family had very limited memorable moments and a plethora of sad moments in life. Currently, his wife is dead and his daughter is living without a mother.

He has lived all his life in a slum. He just wishes that his child should not live the same way and she gets a good job and a good family in the future. He believes that we should succeed without lying and his message to the government was,

> "*If people like us don't have a document or something for a job instead of depriving us of opportunities, they should understand and help us.*"

I was extremely excited to know his life story but when he told me that he is not educated and he manages his grocery with difficulty, I felt guilty as I waste too much food on dinner. Also, I learned that because he is poor, very few people respect him and realized that money plays a big role in this world.

CHAPTER TWELVE

LIVING ON PENNIES

-By Vishal Kumbhar

On the lookout for potential humans to interview, I along with my friends started roaming around, after our school got over. After some time, I saw a family on the footpath. In the hot sun, they were selling garbage bags. They were wearing torn clothes and the children were fighting to eat from one packet of chips. No one was buying their bags and no one was happy among them. Watching this I felt very sad and pity for them. I felt that I should interview them for my project. I went to talk to them, asked them for some time and we started talking about his life.

His name was Mr. S. He had three members in his family: a wife, son, and daughter. Later he said, "We don't really know where we have specifically come from because my parents died when I was young and from that time only I have been doing this business of selling garbage bags. My situation forced me to work at a younger age and therefore I had to leave my school in between."

He needs to change places for selling his material. Every day they hardly get money for their food but the worst time in his life was the pandemic because the whole world was under lockdown and because of it, there was no one to buy his bags. In those days, his family had to starve for 2-3 days.

First, he used to sell these bags in Kharadi, but no one used to buy them there, so he came here to Mundhwa signal. Again, it's the same here. Not many people buy bags from him. He only gets 30-50 rupees profit every day. Most of the time people bargain so he sometimes earns even less than that. He continued, "We can't reject them also because we already have very few customers."

One of the things he wanted to tell society,

"*When you buy something from a mall, then you won't do any bargaining, but when it comes to us, it changes. Please don't do it with us, we need to work every day for food and in that also we need to sacrifice our money.*"

Many times his condition forces his child to beg for food. It was really sad to see his family in these conditions. His message was completely sensible and relatable. Every day we buy lots of things and we do bargaining only with poor vendors. Now I am realizing how unfair it is!

Thus, I have decided to buy things mostly from roadside vendors and not bargain with them. This would help them get some extra profit and improve their financial condition. And hopefully, they will be happy.

CHAPTER THIRTEEN

DIGNITY IS A LUXURY

-By Pushpa Ram

Interaction with Ms. A

I remember when I was returning home from school and I saw a lady. She was selling tea. I thought to myself "Why not talk to her and know more about her?". I went near her and asked if she would like to talk to me in regards to my Project. She agreed and I started my conversation with her.

Her name was Ms. A. She was 50 years. She had come to Pune from Solapur. Currently, she sells tea at the roadside of Mundhwa, Pune. While she was talking to me, I was able to recognize her tension by her expressions and words. She was in a hurry as it was her work time.

She told me about her childhood that she had only studied till grade 5 and after that, she didn't go to school. Then she was married off. After her marriage, she had 2 daughters and 1 son. Unfortunately, her husband met with an accident and that moment was the worst moment of her life, she said. She urgently needed 1- 2 lakhs for her husband's treatment. She went to the bank to ask for a loan, but they refused. She also made police complaints but she did not receive any kind of help after that as well.

Because of all these irregularities, her husband passed away. While sharing this, her eyes were full of tears and her pain was visible. She said that it's difficult for her to manage her money as her expenditure is quite higher than the revenue she earns.

I asked her "Why don't you try working somewhere else?". She replied that she tried, but didn't find any kind of job, as she is not educated. People always rejected her from giving any kind of job. She said that in the morning, she opens her tea stall and she earns mediocre money. She charges 10 rupees per cup. She told me that she never feels safe, as sometimes people talk very rudely with her. She said that she doesn't expect anything from the government but she does expect only one thing from society and that is respect. She said,

"I only want respect. I can earn money from my own small tea shop and this tea shop is my everything, my life, my everything."

I thanked her and I am willing to help her in some way. I felt as if little courage has transferred from her soul to mine. Also, I learned how difficult it is to conduct a small business and how difficult it is to be the sole earner for the family. She works no lesser than any other working human but we as a society always give respect based on the economic status of another human.

CHAPTER FOURTEEN

LIFE OF LONELINESS

-By Vrushabh Gawade

On my way back from school, I always observe a homeless man who sits down on the bridge near the Hadapsar railway station. I thought of taking his interview. When I approached him, he was wearing ragged clothes. I nervously went ahead with a fear of whether he would shout or hit me, so to ease the situation I bought him a Vada Pav to eat. He was very happy to see the food, and looking at that I slipped the question, "Bhaiya, Could you please share with me your life story?"

It is extremely difficult to get to know these men. Their brutal public life is encased in a hard shell. His name was Mr. K. He lived alone since he was 4 years old when his father and mother died. No one accepted him in his family because they believed they would not keep a burden on their head. It was extremely difficult for him to stay alone. Later, he learned to stay alone. He was not educated. It was difficult for him to survive. He wanted to study as a child. He used to see some of his friends who used to go to school, but unfortunately, he couldn't go. As he grew up, he realized that he needed to do some jobs to survive and get food. However, he failed. He went through multiple health issues. He lived in Solapur before but he understood that a setting like this won't help him to grow up. So he came to Pune. He started by begging here but he didn't get to eat food even once a day with that money, so after multiple challenging circumstances, he eventually got a job in a railway station. There he just earned 50 rupees a day which was not at all enough. Then he changed his job to being a sweeper which was better to be able to survive.

After some years, he got married. Happiness had finally arrived in his life. Both of them supported each other to grow in their lives. They believed that when you direct your attention to things you are passionate about, you feel more positive and motivated. When you have positivity in your life, happiness isn't far away. A few years later, his wife was pregnant. He was filled with happiness. But, it didn't last long. When it was time for delivery, he lost his wife and his child. He was broken badly and sorrow again returned to his life.

Once again he became alone and he went into depression and was broken mentally. He cried a lot. He got addicted to alcohol & tobacco. His days passed in depression. But he realized that to come out of those situations, he needed to make efforts now. He believed that God never sends more challenges for one person than he can handle. The realization of it didn't make him happy, but he had a clear horizon opening in front of him, free from the rainy curtains and filled with the sunny light of awareness. He is still in the hope that his good time is yet to arrive again.

Finally, he just had one message to society,

"Parents are the greatest gift for anyone. I was unlucky that no one was there to nurture me, but those who have it, do give them the utmost respect they deserve."

I was dumbstruck after this experience. I could imagine the amount of pain and loneliness he goes through as I have lost my father too. I and my friends used to tease him with the name '*Aeda*' (Mental) but this experience made me empathize with him and know his side of the story. We sometimes judge people by their actions and don't even try to understand the 'Why' of their actions. It opened my eyes and I will encourage everyone to be more humane with these people as they need it the most!

CHAPTER FIFTEEN

IMPORTANCE OF THE EDUCATION

-By Tejaswee Hole & Prajakta Gaud

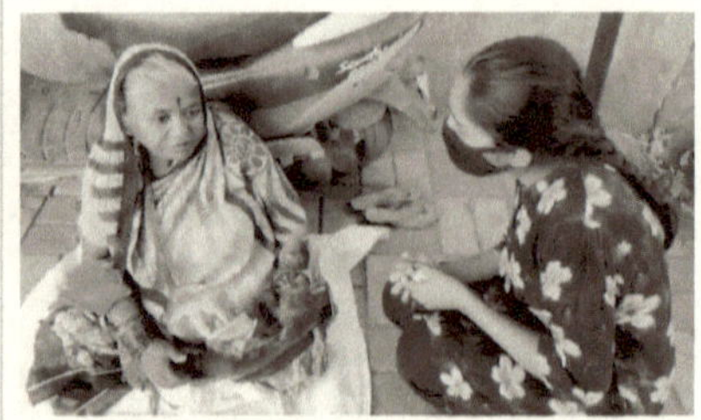

Interaction with Ms. K

A few days ago, we saw one old woman on the Mundhwa footpath in Pune. She was selling garbage bags. She looked quite dull & tense, so we decided to talk with her. We went to her and asked her, "Could we speak with you?". She readily agreed and we started talking.

Her name was Ms. K and she was from Pandharpur. Her childhood was not very good because her family's economic conditions were not good. They had to suffer for food as well. As it was very hard for her parents to handle two daughters, her parents arranged a match for her.

She got married at the age of 10 to a boy who was 8 years older than her. She gave birth to a baby boy at the age of 15. At the same time, her father passed away, and around 3-4 years later, her mother also passed away. Those were the worst days for her as she had lost her backbone of support.

So she shifted to Pune in search of a job, as she had heard, Pune is a developed city in Maharashtra. She thought it wouldn't be hard to get a job in Pune. But actually, she was not educated enough, so she didn't get any job. Going back to Pandharpur was no longer the way for her as she had lost her biological mother and father.

Somehow she started selling small-small things like flowers, garbage bags, pens, etc. Later she took one small house on rent of Rs 2500 per month for her family. But still, she didn't have enough money to send her son to school. She used to get only 20-30 rupees profit. Unfortunately, her son was forced to help her in selling these items due to her circumstances.

But the worst time was lockdown. In 2020, the virus called Covid-19 was spreading everywhere and led to the whole world being under lockdown. And her financial condition was so bad that if she didn't earn for a single day, her family would not get food on their plates, so in lockdown, she had to beg for her family.

Also, she said that when they started begging and selling these bags, she used to feel very disrespected and dejected because people used to comment on them and treat them very badly. But now she doesn't feel anything as she has got accustomed to listening to those comments.

But the sad thing was even her small innocent son needed to face all these things. So when he reached the age of 21, she found a match for her son and married him. Now she has one granddaughter and a grandson. But they all are suffering through poverty. If they won't work for even a single day, they won't get food that day.

The only thing she wishes is to see her granddaughter and grandson study. Because if they get an education they will get a secure and stable future. We asked her, "What message would you like to give to society?" She replied,

"Don't leave your school in between because the basis of a stable life is education. If you are educated you can achieve whatever you want."

At last, we realized that she didn't have much but she had hope whereas we have lots of opportunities to do so many things, but we don't take them seriously and give up on them, but now we understand that we need to deep dive into studies with dedication and do something for ourselves and our parents to make everyone feel proud.

No Tears Left to Cry

-By Nitesh Yadav

I remember, when I was traveling home from school, I saw a man who was sweeping the road. I felt so sad looking at him because he looked too old and weak. I went to him and tried to talk with him, he said, "I do not want to talk to anyone". When I asked, "Why?", he didn't reply. The next day when I was returning home from school, I saw the same person. He was sitting under a tree near drainage and a dirty smell was coming from the drain. Then again I tried to talk to him. He replied, "What will you do after knowing my problems and about me?" I politely responded, "I will try to help you by writing your story." He knew that I'm young and by seeing my kind heart, he agreed to tell me about his life.

His name was Mr. R and he was born in Uttar Pradesh in the small village of Aavari. His mother passed away when she gave birth to him. He was married at the age of 15 years only. His father was badly addicted to smoking and alcohol and thus in 2002, his father passed away. He was broken from the bottom of his heart. His childhood was painful and lacked happiness. He didn't have his land for agriculture in the village and thus didn't understand what to do? So, he decided to come to Pune in search of a job and a better future along with his wife.

In 2003, he came to Pune. After much struggle, he eventually found a job as a household helper. He worked there for 6 months before the owner of the job removed him by saying, "You are a thief and you have stolen my mobile." The owner didn't even give him the full salary. Mr. R wasn't able to do anything. He went into depression. He was in the search of a new job, but he didn't get a job easily.

In 2006, his wife got pregnant. Both of them were delighted after the news but also worried as they didn't have any stable jobs. And in the very same year, Doctors asked them to do a cesarean delivery, but due to lack of money, her wife's operation could not be done and that child died during normal delivery. They were devasted. The only hope of happiness also vanished before reaching their helpless hands.

Mr. R continued searching but didn't get any job. So, he started begging on the streets. Sometimes he used to get some food or money but sometimes for 3 continuous days, he didn't get anything from begging. So for 3 days he and his wife used to survive by only drinking water. One day when he was begging, the police came and started abusing him. Then one sensible Policeman asked him, "Why are you begging?" He told everything about his life. Understanding the gravity of the situation, the Policeman arranged a job of sweeping for him.

Till now, Mr. R is doing the same work of sweeping in Mundhwa and earning decent money. When I asked him, "What do you want from the government and what message do you want to give to society?" Then he replied,

"I only want respect and help from society during difficult times. And from the government, I want some facilities from which our life could become a little easier."

From his life experience, I have learned that only poor people can understand the value of privilege in life, as they have none. Mr. R and his wife have gone through so many struggles and so much amount of pain that they can handle. And it is fair to say that they don't have any more tears left to cry!

CHAPTER SEVENTEEN

ZINDAGI EK SUFFER

-By Vidhi Bagade

Interaction with Ms. R

When I was walking back to my home from school, I saw that a lady was selling bangles on the street. I observed her for a long time because most people were ignoring her when she was asking them to buy bangles. When I went to her, she told me, "Dear, please buy some bangles from me. It would be great. I will earn something." I was just quiet for some time. I had no words to say. After some time, I told her, "Okay, give me those small size bangles." The happiness which I saw on her face was precious. I asked, "Ma'am, would you talk to me for 10 minutes?" After hearing the word Ma'am from me, she felt happy and respected and she agreed to talk.

I asked her, "Could you please tell me about your life?" She said "Yes", but she was a little nervous. I told her that it is a free and open space and nothing to be nervous about. She felt better and we continued. Her name was Ms. R. She stays in Pune with her family. She has 2 daughters and one son and her husband is an alcoholic. She told me that she works for 10 hours but she only gains around 100 rupees profit in a day by selling her bangles.

Then I asked, "How do you fulfill your children's needs? Does your husband support you in the upbringing of your children?" She said that she is unable to fulfill her children's needs because of her financial condition. She always tries to fulfill their needs. She said that her husband always snatched her earnings from her to drink alcohol.

When I asked her, "What difficulties do you face while selling these bangles?" She replied to me that people always ignore her and they don't buy bangles from her. She said that people spend more money on the same kind of bangles in the physical stores but they resist buying from her. Her bangles cost only 30- 40 rupees but still, they ignore her or say it's too costly.

She told me how much she suffers each day, but she gains little. She is always trying to make her condition better. The golden message that she wants to give to society is,

> *"Being poor is not a crime that we committed, it's not our fault. I just want respect from society, so that I can live proudly in this society."*

I felt that she was a strong woman who is unbroken and she had a sweet and soft nature while conversing. Respect is something that poor people want and deserve. I hope that her husband could get out of his addiction and contribute equally to their family's progress.

CHAPTER EIGHTEEN

THE INCORRECT PATH

-By Akash Deokar

One day I was eating some food at a food stall when a lady came to the same stall and asked for food saying, "Please give me something to eat, I have been hungry for the last three days". She was looking too tired and weak, so I gave her some food to eat. I realized that one homeless human has collided with me by luck, why not enquire about her life story? So I asked her, "What's the problem, Aunty?" Before I finished my question, she started crying. I consoled her and asked the same question again.

She resisted sharing but after 2 to 3 requests she somehow started sharing her life's story and believe me her story was no less than an old Bollywood movie. Her name was Ms. A and she belonged to a financially well family from Daund, Pune. When she was studying in the first year of senior college, a boy called Harish proposed to her. She readily agreed because she also loved him.

Somehow, this news reached her father. Her father called her back from college immediately and asked her to marry his friend's son named Sagar. She disagreed. Her father tried to force her, but she didn't agree. She only wanted to marry Harish. She requested her father but he didn't listen.

At last, she got angry and said, "If I won't marry Harish then I will not marry anyone else." Her father gave a condition to her that if she wanted to live in his house, then she needed to marry Sagar. If she doesn't want to marry Sagar, then she can leave the house forever. She agreed and left her parental house and went to Harish. What she saw at Harish's house was life-changing. It was a suicidal situation.

She saw Harish with his wife. She shockingly asked, "What is this Harish?" Harish didn't reply and very disrespectfully pulled her out of his house and life.

She was completely broken. However, now her eyes were open. When she went back to her father saying that she will marry Sagar, it was already too late. Her father refused to accept her.

From that day onwards she started begging. I asked her if she wanted to give any message to society, then she replied,

> *"Just listen to your parents because they know way more than you. If they are telling you anything then there must be some reason, so please respect it."*

I never imagined that a Bollywood story could happen with someone in real life. I wanted to know, why on this earth would she choose to beg at such an early age, but she just left and I was contemplating that something deep must be hidden behind her aching eyes.

CHAPTER NINETEEN

Society Is Selfish

-By Amit Sharma

Interaction with Mr. R

While searching for homeless humans, I saw a man sitting near the road. He was packed from head to toe with his white Raincoat and had a black bag on his shoulders. From his decent condition, I was a little confused about whether he is homeless or not. To know answers to my questions, I thought about talking to him and registering his struggles and sufferings if any, for my story. I went to him and asked him if he would like to talk to me and share his life story with me, thankfully he agreed to talk to me and we started the conversation.

His name was Mr. R. He admitted that currently he is homeless, but before being homeless, he had a good life. Everything in his life was going good and well, but one day shockingly his father died in an accident. His mother was not strong enough to bear the sadness of her husband's death, so she committed suicide. After traveling from the village, Uncle R came to Pune with some hope in his heart.

In Pune, he struggled a lot to get work. He didn't even have a home. Without money, surviving is difficult in this world. So he started to beg. He said that he never wanted to do this kind of thing, but he was in such a bad condition that he had no options left other than begging. After begging he used to get 20-30 rupees per day. He wanted to study more, but as his financial status was not good, he had to do all this kind of work. After living in Pune for 5 months, he knew all the places and different areas. He started to work in a cycle repairing store and started to earn 3000-4000 rupees per month.

He made few friends and started to live at one of his friend's houses. His friend's parents allowed him to live with them. He said that his friend's parents didn't treat him properly as he was very poor. Sometimes, they even snatched his salary. They didn't give him good food to eat, but he was still tolerating all of these things because he didn't have any other option.

After being taunted for a few months, he decided to leave his friend's house. The owner of the cycle store accused him of stealing money, so he fired Uncle R from the cycle store. The situation was getting difficult for him, so again he started to beg. Now everyone calls him 'Bevda' (alcoholic). He is spending his current life begging and he only prays to God that no one should get a life like him. During the Corona pandemic, he didn't have enough food, so sometimes he was starving or he was going to Kodre Hospital in Mundhwa, just to get some food to eat.

At last, he had only one message to say,

> "*This society is very selfish. They don't understand others' problems. If I could get a good job somewhere, I would be ready to work with honesty and integrity. Even if I get less money, I am completely okay, but I just want some respect so that I can live with dignity in this society.*"

I realized how difficult it gets when parents leave us early. Also, how money could make humans do things that they never imagined. His story was tragic but still, I think he could do much better in life if he tries hard enough. Alcohol addiction could test our ability to be resilient.

CHAPTER TWENTY

GIVEN UP ON LIFE

-By Sumit Nath

When I was walking on the footpath, I came across a beggar. When I saw him, I remembered my English project. I convinced him to give an interview and started diving deep into his childhood.

His name was Mr. V. He had a good family and used to live with his grandfather and three more siblings. They had a lot of farming land where they grew many things like wheat, daal, sugarcane, etc. After some years his grandfather died, so everyone decided to divide the property into equal parts.

When his siblings were dividing the property, they fought with him and didn't give him any property. They used to give him just some food to eat every day, but it was not enough for him to live his life the way he wanted. Thus he left that house and went to Mumbai. In Mumbai, he lived with his friends and worked as a carpenter. He earned 5-6 thousand rupees per month but that didn't suffice for the electricity bill, house rent, groceries, etc.

He again left that home as well and came to Pune. In Pune, he didn't know anyone, that's why he ate leftover food from hotels. He used to sleep in the Government Electric Generator room. No one was allowed in that room, so he used to go there secretly. Some days passed like this, but one day a Police Officer saw him and beat him a lot. After this, he lost hope and decided to beg on the streets.

Later I asked him, "What help do you want from the government? " He replied that he doesn't want anything because he thinks that there is nothing left in his life. The only thing he wanted to say was,

> *"Please ask people's compulsion behind doing some illegal things before punishing them."*

I tried to motivate him to find a carpenter job in Pune and be free from the life of poverty but his eyes lacked any desire to change his situation. Probably the mental trauma was prohibiting him from taking any action or not having anyone for emotional support made him give up on himself.

STRUGGLES OF LIFE

-By Naziya Shaikh

Interaction with Ms. S

When I was returning home with my friend, I saw one lady on the road. No one was helping her. I decided to interview her for my English Project. I went near her to learn more about her life. I asked her, "Could I get a few minutes to talk?" She said, "Yes Dear, You can. But what will you achieve by talking to me?" I explained my project in brief and we started our conversation.

Her name was Ms. S. In her family, there is her husband, 2 daughters, and a son. All of them used to live in a rented house but one day her husband got a paralysis attack and most of his body got paralyzed. He was neither able to walk nor talk. Tears start rolling her eyes while sharing this incident. She tried to treat her husband but there was no improvement. Their savings got vanished and ultimately they were thrown out of the rented house. Without realizing it, they were homeless. As she was uneducated, it was really hard for her to get any job.

All of them started living on the footpath and it was uncomfortable at first but now they have got accustomed to it. Her children did not go to school. She knew that she was destroying her kids' future but her kids understood her problems and never blamed her for it. Two of her daughters got married to some far-off relatives, so only her son and her husband are left with her as of now. Her husband still doesn't do any work as he is paralyzed. She and her son sell toys and also beg throughout the day and they only earn around 50-70 rupees which is not enough to fill everyone's stomach in the family, so sometimes her family doesn't get any food to eat.

She has been trying to find another job for a long time but she is not getting one. I asked her if the government or I can help her in any way. She said, "Yes" with all her hope.

She continued,

> *"I want to leave begging. I am ready to work harder than I do. If I and my son could get a job to earn enough money, then we all could live happily and my son won't have to suffer like me in the future."*

I thanked her for giving me her precious time. Again and again, her story and her suffering were coming to my mind. I realized that the struggles faced by us shape the person we become. We should be thankful for the hard times as they can only make us stronger. Also, I pray that Ms. S situation should get better soon and I wish that our society would show its humanity.

CHAPTER TWENTY-TWO

LIFE FLIPS IN FEW SECONDS

-By Vedant Pawar

There were lots of things around my house but what I remember is one small paan shop near my house. Every day I used to see the shopkeeper who always looked tense. He looked like a 21-22-year-old sitting inside the shop and thinking about something.

I decided to take his interview for my English Project. So I went near him and called him. In the first attempt, he didn't listen, then the second time I was loud and called him, then he listened to me and asked me, "What do you want?" In a silent voice, I asked him, "What is the reason that you are looking so tense?" When I asked him this question, he became uncomfortable and said, "Nothing. Tell me what do you want?" I knew that there was a reason that he was not ready to speak up, but I didn't give up and asked him with dignity, "I am not connected to you with blood, but as a human, you can talk with me and lessen the burden of your worries." I think he liked my tone, so he agreed and started his introduction from childhood.

His name was Mr. G. In childhood, he lived in a village and completed his education there. When he grew up, he came to the city to find some work and earn money. He was unaware of the city environment, culture and conditions. But still, he never gave up and continued searching for a job. For 2 days his search didn't lead to any outcome but on the 3rd day, he finally got a decent job. He started working at a factory that made biscuits. He used to get a good salary there, around 24,000 Rupees per month.

However, luck was not with him. That company only functioned for 6 months and shut down for some reason. So he again started searching for a job, but he was only getting failures. Mr. G was tired of searching for jobs, so he decided to open his own business. He saw an advertisement that there was a small shop available for 2000 Rs per month. He contacted the shop owner and finally set up his shop and started selling Paan-related items, but the net earnings were not so good. It was not sufficient for him because he had to give shop rent, and home rentals and also had to send money to the village for his parents.

I said that all of this is very difficult but time will change soon, the situation will get better but his reply shocked me because he said that his father has a medical emergency and they need money for treatment but he has no money for them. He was feeling ashamed of himself. He said,

> *"I am able to see this beautiful world because of them, but I am not able to help them when they are in need."*

I felt helpless after hearing this. Later I asked him if he wanted any help from the government, then he replied that it would be a big favor if the government provided some financial help for his father's operation. With that, I closed my interview wishing him the best of luck with his father's operation.

I learned that life does not stay the same forever and also we should cherish whatever we currently possess because **the life we are living might be a dream for someone else.**

CHAPTER TWENTY-THREE

LIFE OF SELF-RESPECT

-By Mayuresh Kamble

Interaction with Mr. V

Near the Mundhwa area, there is one tea stall and I have seen one man working over there. He always seems to be nervous and fearful, so I thought of taking his interview. I went there and requested him whether I could conduct his interview for a project in the school. He agreed. At first, he was scared because he didn't know what is the interview? But I explained to him that I will just ask a few questions and needed a few answers. He calmed down a little and I started asking about his life.

His name was Mr. V. He washes utensils for a living. When he washes 10 dishes, he gets 1 cup of tea and when he washes all day, then only he gets to eat food 2 times. When asked about his childhood, he replied that it was not at all good because when he was young, his parents passed away. He became an orphan at a very young age and does not remember his parents. The owner of the tea stall only gave him a job and a place to sleep.

He lives alone and has two-three friends. All of his friends thought of begging to earn some money and eat food but he didn't want to beg because he believes that he has body parts intact to do a job. That's why he continued working in this tea stall.

His dream was to be a Police Officer because he wanted to help his country but he didn't have money to study, so he wasn't able to fulfill his dream. I asked him, "If I will give you a job to do, then would you accept it?" He said, "I will not go anywhere from here, I will wash dishes but I will not go anywhere else."

At last, I asked him, "What kind of help do you want from the government?" He said,

> *"I want Government to instruct the Police to not beat beggars without any crime because whenever at night, the beggar roams around, the Police beats them and pushes them away. I know this because my friends have suffered this."*

This experience gave me an understanding of what struggle really means. I learned that we need to help homeless people, as they too have feelings and they are also part of our society. We can't rely on the Government to help everyone. We need to figure out some solution as a society, for them. Thus, I have decided to give him food whenever I see him.

CHAPTER TWENTY-FOUR

DISREGARDED BY LOVED ONES

-By Buddha Jyoti Gautam

I asked, "Why do you beg?" He replied, "Because I don't have any house or money." Then I asked, "Why don't you do any work?", then he answered that his leg is paralyzed, so he is not able to do any kind of labor work as well. I felt quite dejected by listening to that response. These were a few pieces of the conversation I had with a person, who was begging in front of my father's shop and I thought about having a conversation with him for my English Project.

His name was Mr. V. He lived in Uttar Pradesh in his childhood. He studied till 8th grade only. Later he got married and had 2 children. When his wife died, he was thrown out of his own house by his son. His son didn't want to take care of him, as a lot of money was going to the hospital for his treatment. His son got frustrated and left him. He made sure his son had the best, even when he was at his worst. He sacrificed his sleep so that his son could dream big. He took care of his son when he was sick but this is how he was repaid by him. He was broken and dejected by seeing his son's behavior.

He was in a lot of pain because he also had a wound on his leg. He still couldn't walk properly, so I asked, "Why don't you get your leg operated on?" He laughed and told me, "I don't even get money for food, how would I get the operation done?" I didn't understand how to reply to him. I felt helpless at that moment.

Even though he was paralyzed and badly hurt, he wanted to do a job to survive. He made himself strong and every day he went out in search of a job. He was the most courageous person that I've ever seen. After so many struggles, he wanted to live his life. He was always able to control his circumstances and was able to respond to them. He decided to live his life and defeat his problems.

I remembered one quote after listening to his life experiences. It says,

> "*When life seems unbearable, hold on, because you have not yet seen the next page of the book of life. It is full of unknown mysteries, suspense, adventures, and unachieved success.*"

Along with the respect for Mr. V, I simultaneously had anger toward his child. Our parents nourish us right from day one on this planet, till we become able and do not leave our side but he left Mr. V. I am never going to leave my parents and always provide the care and support as they did for me.

Part 4: Family, a Motivation

CHAPTER TWENTY-FIVE

Happiness in What You Possess

-By Praniti Kapure

Interaction with Ms. S

We are living our lives happily, but still, we want more. We expect better things from our life. We don't value what we have. This understanding got solidified when I met with a human recently. She didn't have anything(*worldly possessions*) in her life but still, she was content with her family.

I saw her begging on the footpath with her husband and her children when I was crossing the Mundhwa signal. I thought of interviewing her for my Project. I approached her and asked, *"Didi, kya aap 10 minute ke liye baat kar sakte hain?* (Sister, Could you please talk with me for 10 minutes?)"* She was very kind and she agreed.

Her name was Ms. S. Her childhood was normal, neither too sad nor too good. She was from Pandharpur. She belonged to a poor family. She didn't get a chance to study, because her parents were from a poor family and they were not capable of paying that much. She had one sister who was also not educated like her. When she became an adult, her parents got her married.

Now she has 2 sons. They are very young. They don't have a home. They beg on signals, sell garbage bags or sometimes they get some flowers from which they make garlands and sell. She still lives with her sister in Pune.

They struggle a lot to get food, clothes, and other basic needs. Her children were very hungry and they didn't have any money and documents to send them to school. Before coming to Pune, she went to Mumbai for a better opportunity but ended up begging. And according to law, begging is an offense, so Police used to abuse them, and thus they came to Pune for a better prospect. Now they live in Pune, sell garbage bags and flower garlands, and beg.

She told me that she feels very dejected when she begs and lives on footpaths. Her children are not educated and it's a very tough life. The message she gave was that the government should give some facilities to beggars so they can at least survive. She said that the Government doesn't give them any facilities and they don't even let them beg. Still, they try to live happily with their family and she said,

"It's okay if I don't have any money or house, but my family is my strength. Together we fight the daily battles and somehow enjoys the small-small things in life."

I learned that I have everything but still I expect more from my mother. I realized the privilege of having 4 walls around me, which I call home. And from now onwards, I will start valuing the things I possess!

CHAPTER TWENTY-SIX

SURVIVOR

-By Prachi Wade

When I was walking down the road, I saw a woman sweeping the road. She was looking weak and tired. I was observing her actions, after sweeping a portion of the road, she sat down. Then I thought, I should talk to her. I walked toward her and offered my water bottle. She drank the water as if she had been thirsty for days. I asked her, "Could I sit next to you?" She said, "Yes, why not". Then I asked her, "Could I take your interview because in school the teacher had given us a project of taking interviews of underprivileged humans?" She agreed after a few seconds of pondering.

I asked about her life. She said that her name was Ms. L and she was 40 years old. She has 2 sons and 1 daughter. She lives in a rented house. It's a single room. Her husband recently got paralyzed, that's why he stays at home. Her son is 19 years old, he was also doing sweeping work before. He used to clean during the day and study at night. Currently, he is working in a hospital. She further told me that she and her son, both are supporting their family financially.

She was 18 years old when she got married whereas her husband was 30 years old at that time. For the money, her family married her off. She wanted to become an IAS officer, but no one supported her and her dream is still a dream. She had a stepmother, her name was Kavita. She was a very rude and selfish woman. She also had 2 daughters. But she kept Ms. L as her maid. She told me that her stepmother never asked her daughters to work. All work was done by Ms. L.

After marriage, her husband got arrested in a case of robbery. Her husband's name was Dhananjay. He was an alcoholic. When her husband was in jail, no one was there to support her financially or emotionally. She went to her stepmother's home, but she refused to help her. They shooed her away like some beggar was begging in front of her house.

Then she sat on a road and started to weep bitterly. She was thinking to commit suicide. She went to the Railway Station and sat on the Railway track. The train was coming, but the people around saved her. She shouted at them and asked, "Why did you save me? I want to die, no one is there for me!" She started to cry loudly but one woman took Ms. L to her home. Her name was Sushma. She told Ms. L that she is also living alone and has no one. She told her that she is working in a factory. She offered Ms. L to work in the same factory. She agreed and was ready to work with her. She started working with Sushma. She was earning Rs 8000 per month and was living happily. One day, the factory closed because the owner of the factory was going into loss. Again Ms. L lost hope. After this incident, both Sushma and Ms. L started to find jobs. After one week, they got a job washing dishes in a hotel. They were getting Rs 200 per day.

Three weeks later, she returned to her husband's home, searching for him. Her husband was lying on the road, fully drunk. He wasn't able to see and was unable to walk properly. Ms. L took him home and fed her husband and changed his clothes, his clothes were torn. She called Sushma over. Ms. L said to her, "We will stay here, you don't waste your money giving rent, we will stay together" and she introduced Sushma to her husband. At the age of 23, when Ms. L had 2 babies, she was in tension. She was worried about how would she feed her babies alone as her husband was just sitting at home. At that time Shushma consoled her and said, "Don't take tension, I am with you and I will be there for you anytime."

As her babies were growing, Shushma was taking care of them while Ms. L was working. As her husband was an alcoholic, he needed money for drinking. He used to steal money from her purse. When she came to know about this, she started keeping her money in a locker. One day, her husband was searching for money to drink and she asked him, "What are you doing?". He said, "Give me money", and she said, "No, I won't." Then her husband beat her very badly. Ms. L started to cry. Sushma asked her, "What happened, why are you crying?". L said, "I am saving money for my children, but my husband is stealing money from my purse".

Shushma advised her to keep her children in a hostel where they will get a good education and life. She agreed and kept her children in Marutirao Kote Abhinav Public hostel.

After 10 years, she asked her children to drop out of the hostel. She called them home. Her husband started crying on seeing his children. He was missing them a lot. He had been wanting to see them for years. After staying far from his children, he fully changed. He said sorry for his past actions. Recently, Ms. L changed her job and started sweeping. She got her husband a job too. Both started doing jobs and they were staying happily until her husband got a Paralysis attack and again she got alone. This time her elder son supported her with the work and finances of the family.

I got very emotional after listening to her story. In the end, I asked her, What message do you want to give society?" She said,

> *"After eating chocolates or anything, please throw the waste in the dustbin. Don't throw it on the road. We can't sweep it for hours and hours. We are also humans, we too have feelings. We also get tired by sweeping the road."*

After listening to her, I also started to throw the waste in the dustbin. Before, I was throwing plastics on the road. Also, I learned that there were so many ups and downs in her life, but she was able to survive the situation with the help of friends and family. Having a group of people around, who understands you and comforts you in the difficulties of life is "**Real Gold**".

CHAPTER TWENTY-SEVEN

THE FATHER'S DESTINATION

-By Aaniya Shaikh

Interaction with Mr. B

On my way to school, I occasionally observe one Cobbler Uncle on the roadside. He sets up his shop with all his tools spread around that little region. He was fixing the slippers, when I went near him and asked, "Uncle, Could I talk with you for 10 minutes? I want to take your interview". Then Uncle was a little surprised at first and replied, "Strange! But what do you want to know about me?" with a little smile on his face. Then I explained to him a few questions about his childhood, struggles, and current life, which I would ask and we started interacting.

The Uncle's name was Mr. B and he was 45 years old. He was quite tall. He came to Pune 10 years ago around the year 2010. He used to live in Beed city in his childhood which is 5-6 hrs away from Pune. He was educated only till 5th grade. He did not study further because his family could not afford it.

He came to Pune and opened a shop. He has been doing cobbler work for the past 10 years. He was married and had two daughters and one son. His elder daughter is married and his son is studying in college. They had a plethora of problems due to Coronavirus and had to struggle in Lockdown. Whatever money they had made got finished in lockdown. He was afraid and flabbergasted to see this. If the lockdown was imposed again, they might have to starve and struggle. Taking this as an inspiration, he started working harder now.

Uncle has been working very hard for his son's education. He wants to see him triumph in his life. His only aim is to see his son happy and accomplished. He wants help from the government in terms of extra educational support so that his son can get a government job after his graduation.

Uncle needs help from society to motivate, inspire and appreciate his son. He wants to make good judgments because he doesn't want his son's motivation to go down mid-way and instead wants to give him strength. This cobbler as a father gave his son the greatest gift anyone could give another person- he believed in his son's strength. His son understood the struggle that his father is going through, so he has started studying harder now. His son pledged to make his father proud and he is wishing for his son's happiness and success. He said,

> "*Fathers are wonderful in a million different ways, and they always deserve loving compliments and lots of praise. I'm very at ease, and I like it. I never thought I would be such a family-oriented person. I didn't think, that was part of my makeup. But somebody said that as you get older you become the person you always should have been, and I feel that's happening to me. I'm rather surprised at who I am, because I'm actually like my dad.*"

I was really impressed by the dedication of Uncle toward his son's education and how he was working hard for his family. In the whole conversation, he never showed that he was victimized by the circumstances and showed the mindset of accepting the challenges of life. Having the mindset of a challenger would be the biggest learning for me.

CHAPTER TWENTY-EIGHT

A Strong Independent Woman

-By Dyaneshwari Gaikwad

One day when I was traveling on the road, I saw one woman, who was sitting on the road with a vegetable cart beside her. I felt very sad after seeing her in that condition as her Saree was torn and it was too dirty. I went there and tried to talk to her. When I requested her to take her interview, she replied, "Yes, you can take it but what will you do with it?". Then I replied, "I will write your life story". Then she agreed and I started asking about her childhood life.

Her name was Ms. K and she was from Shirdi. Her dream was to become a Doctor and help everyone but it never got realized because when she was young, her parents passed away. Her near relatives took care of her. She remained uneducated and just learned household work.

Later, she got married at the age of 19 years. Her relationship with her husband was not strong as a lot of quarrels used to happen because of his drinking habit. Somehow, she managed the stress and lived with it.

After a few years, she gave birth to a baby girl and named her 'Bhagyalaxmi'. Ms. K gave utmost attention to her and pledged to fulfill all her dreams. But one unfortunate incident took place, her husband died due to liver failure. She felt helpless and went into the trauma of how she would take care of her daughter alone. But she held herself up and came to Pune only to make her daughter's future bright.

Currently, her daughter is studying in 6th grade in a government hostel and she proudly said that her daughter's dream is to become a Police Officer and help everyone. She further said that for the last many days, she didn't see her daughter because she didn't have money to visit her. But she is happy that she has been able to provide education to her beloved daughter.

She also told me about her life and how she struggles every day. She sells vegetables on 6 days of the week and on Monday, she sells flowers to worshippers. Sometimes she doesn't get enough food to eat, so she fills her stomach by drinking water and sleeping. When I asked her, "What do you expect from the government?" She said that she only wants the government to help her daughter by making her dream come true.

From this story, I learned that if a mother is determined, then she could go to any extent to fulfill the dream of her child. Ms. K left her native place and came to Pune all alone, just to give better education to her child and that is highly commendable!

CHAPTER TWENTY-NINE

ENORMOUS GRIT OF A WOMAN

-By Tanishka Jadhav

Interaction with Ms. R

I remember, while my friends and I were looking for humans to interview, we saw a man and woman sitting beside each other and selling flower garlands on the footpath. One of my friends went to interview the man and I went toward the woman. During the interaction only, I realized that they are husband and wife. Her husband's story and perspective about life have been covered by my friend Yana Ghumle in the previous chapter '*The Struggles and Growth of a Man*'.

Coming on to her story. Her name was Ms. R and when I asked, "How was your childhood?" She replied that her childhood was painful and full of struggles. There were a plethora of difficult circumstances since she was born. Her parents tried to get some jobs, but unfortunately, they didn't have any jobs to do. She didn't get any education, because the family couldn't afford it. At the age of 20 years, she got married. After marriage, she realized one of her hidden talents- making garlands. So, she started making flower garlands. She worked day and night making garlands and started making some money with her husband. Currently, she has two kids.

She never got an education in her childhood, but she wants to give education to her children because she knew that education helps to build character as we learn about different cultures, languages, and how other people think as well as live. But it was not easy for her to put her children into school. There were various obstacles on the way. She needed several types of documents in the admission process. It was truly tough for her and she was wholeheartedly broken. She had pledged to herself that her children would get an education. She had to go to various government offices to make documents. But she was not someone who could break easily. Eventually, after a long wait, she was able to provide all the documents she needed. Hence, she gave the documents for the admission process and now her elder child goes to a government school.

She told me about her job, which was making flower garlands and selling them on a footpath. She was even struggling in that job. She wasn't able to make enough money from it. She and her husband could hardly earn enough for their family to survive. But she never gave up. Instead, she faced her problems and chased them away. She continued,

> *"I always worked hard for all the situations which came my way, because I want to see my children happy and educated. Our society should learn to be benevolent & give respect to every person whether it is big or small."*

I realized that mothers don't make a big deal out of it, but they have plenty of struggles that they keep to themselves. Mothers make every effort to make their child one in a million and sacrifice every comfort of their life for the comfort of their child. From this experience, I got to understand my own mother better and my respect for her increased by multi-folds.

CHAPTER THIRTY

The Dedicated Life

-By Rachana Mali

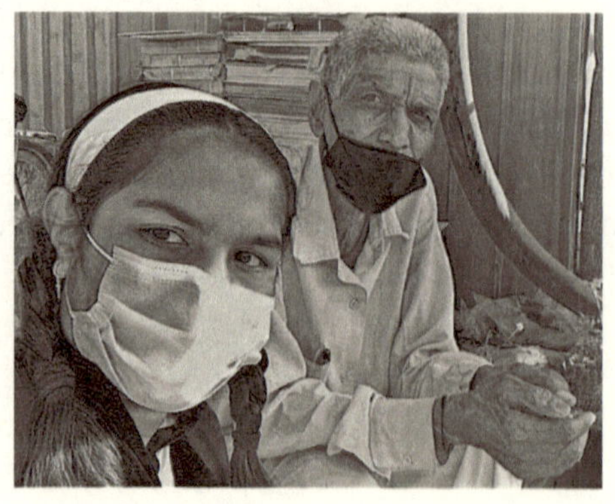

Interaction with Mr. S

One day I went out to buy some bananas and just a little distance from the market, one *Dadaji* (Grandfather) was selling bananas. He was sweating a lot as it was a sunny day and he was selling bananas in this hot climate without any shelter.

First I felt sympathetic for him and then decided to interview him for my project. So I went to buy bananas from him. I bought 1 dozen bananas and gave him a 200 rupee note, then he said, "Beta, I am here since morning but no one has bought bananas yet. You are my first customer so I don't have any change." Then I found a change from a nearby shop and asked him for some time to take his interview. He pointed to one small iron sheet house on his backside colony and asked me to come later. I agreed and went back to meet him in the evening.

As we both started our conversation I asked him to share about his life and also about his childhood. He told me his name was Mr. S and he had studied till 3rd grade. In his time 3rd grade was the highest education in his village. As he completed his 3rd grade, he started working on a farm with his father and after two to three years, he got married to a girl named Suman.

Later the couple gave birth to a baby girl. When his girl grew a little older, Mr. S father passed away because of a heart attack. As he was having one younger brother, legally they needed to do property division. They proceeded with land division and he continued to do farming to survive. When his girl 'Siddhi' became 18 years old, they came to Pune for her education.

In the 21st century, his education was having very low value, so he sold his farm in Kolhapur, bought a fruit stall, and started selling fruits. They were living in a small 1RK house and 5 years later, he & his wife found a match for his daughter and married her in Mumbai.

As he had to spend lots of money on his daughter's wedding, he sold his fruits shop. After he sold his fruits shop, it was very hard for him to survive for 4-5 months, thus his daughter came forward to help him with money.

With time, he found some irritation in Siddi's behavior and he understood the cause of it and asked her daughter to not send any more money to him and his daughter easily accepted. It was clearly understood that Siddhi was not caring about how her parents will survive. Later, he took a loan and bought one cart which they used to roam everywhere and sell fruits and sometimes vegetables.

Once he was not feeling well, so he decided that he would not go to sell fruits, but his wife Suman said, "We have lots of fruits and if we do not sell them today, then it would go to waste" and she took the cart to sell the fruits. Her husband was stopping her but she did not listen to him. She stepped out and in one hour Mr. S's phone rang, he picked up the phone, and suddenly his world completely turned upside-down. The person who had called him said that one truck had crashed with his wife and their fruit cart and she is admitted to the Government hospital of Mundhwa (Kodre Kutir Hospital).

He immediately went there and he found that his wife had lost one leg forever and she was paralyzed. He was completely broken. Everything was destroyed for him. Now he was expecting that his daughter Siddhi would live with them for some days, but as his daughter was pregnant, her husband did not allow her to live there for more than 2-3 days. He was completely disappointed as he said, "That moment was the biggest heartbreak of my life. My wife and I had dedicated our whole life to our daughter and she was not having a few days for her old parents."

They both somehow managed themselves and stood again. He started selling fruits on footpaths because, in that same accident, his fruit vehicle was also destroyed. Now he is completely hopeless in his life but only for his wife, he is working. Later, I asked him if he wanted any help from the government, then he said,

> *"What will I ask them for? Here my own blood doesn't care for me, what can I expect from strangers? The only message I want to give to the young generation is to please support your parents in their tough times as they did in yours."*

It was a very gloomy state of affairs to hear his story. I resonated with him that it is a really painful feeling when we do everything for someone and they just don't reciprocate the care.

CHAPTER THIRTY-ONE

SACRIFICES FOR CHILDREN

-Interviewed By Aryan Gaikwad & Saurabh Verma
-Collated By Aman Gupta

One day while searching for disadvantaged humans for the interview, Aryan found one Uncle who was sitting in his auto-rickshaw. He looked sad at first glance. Aryan went to him and asked, "Uncle, could I take your interview for 10 minutes?" He agreed hesitantly.

His name was Mr. M. He was born in Solapur. He was 42 years old and was married. He was 8th pass and his dream was to become a Doctor, but because of his family's financial problems, he was not able to study further and his dream was crushed to ashes.

He came to Pune 8 years ago around the year 2013. He struggled to find a job initially but finally settled on a security guard job. But unfortunately, In the lockdown caused by Covid-19, he lost his job and had to find some alternative.

With the help of his friends, he bought an auto-rickshaw using a loan and started serving passengers. In this job, he has to sleep at 12:00 at night and wake up at 4:00 in the morning. Also, the money he earns is quite meager and he is not able to save anything for the future. He does not like his new job but still has to deal with it to survive.

Currently, he lives in a rented house with a rent of Rs 3000 per month. He has 1 daughter and 1 son. They both are studying in a government school and he had one desperate wish for his children, he said,

"I want to see my children in a decent job in the future and be free from the financial crisis which my family faces every single day."

Interaction with Mr. Shree

One fine day when Saurabh was looking for underprivileged humans, he went through a street full of tall buildings and societies. The people were talking, having fun and there he spotted a watchman and Saurabh thought of interacting with him.

His name was Mr. S. He was 62 years old and had less hair. He was from Kerala and came to Pune for a job a long time ago. He had 3 children- 1 girl and 2 boys. All of his children were married and got settled in life. He was living with his wife in a small rented single-room apartment. He said,

"I have spent my whole life earning for my children. I want them to be happy and enjoy the life which my wife and I never got the chance to."

Both of the life experiences tell us that a lot of people lose the hope to achieve their dreams and hope that what they couldn't achieve, would somehow be achieved by their children. They spend their whole life, trying every possible means to give an opportunity to their children, which they never got in their lives. They keep sacrificing for their children and for a lot of them, their children become the motivation to live!

CHAPTER THIRTY-TWO

WAR WITH SITUATIONS

-By Kanchan Kol

Interaction with Ms. G

I remember when I was traveling on the Mundwa Chowk road, I saw many homeless people. They were very weak and looked exhausted. They were sitting on a footpath. Before I used to ignore them and didn't give them any importance, because I used to think that they are uneducated, they were not hardworking and also they don't like to make an effort, that's why they were homeless and beggars. I was thoroughly wrong. They have to struggle so much for every single thing. I felt dejected and got emotional by seeing their kind hearts. Now, I feel empathetic towards them.

I thought of interacting with one of those homeless people. I found a lady named Ms. G. She had 3 children. She had been struggling a lot in her life. She couldn't afford anything for her children. Her children were too innocent and had worn unclean clothes. She didn't want to see her children in such conditions, unfortunately, she wasn't able to fulfill their needs.

She told me that her childhood was painful and filled with difficult circumstances. She wasn't able to go to school, because her parents couldn't afford it and they didn't have jobs. They used to live in a small village. The village people didn't treat them with respect because they were very poor.

Later, Ms. G got married. She and her family came to Mundhwa, Pune to stay. It was not easy for them to stay in Mundhwa. As she and her husband were uneducated, they didn't get any job and they were compelled to beg. Later, they started selling balloons and toys. They had been trying every day to give proper nutrition to their children. One day, her husband broke the bone of his hand. At that time she became weak because both of them have to work hard together for their children's future. She knew that sitting like this won't let her grow. So, she has been trying every day to provide for all the needs of her children. She has been trying to search for jobs. She wants to fulfill her children's needs, makes their dreams come true, and educate them. She is a woman who didn't give up on the situations but she fought with situations. She needs some government support in terms of free education for their children and a home to stay in.

She was quite vocal about her needs and it reminded me of one quote from J.K Rowling which says,

"Help only comes to those who ask for it."

I felt sorry for the problems which they are facing right from early childhood. I learned how to respectfully interact with homeless people. I decided to not throw the remaining food as there are people who can't afford it. Also, I learned determination from her as she was quite stubborn to find better opportunities and give a decent life to her children. I hope that she gets some opportunity in her life to prove herself and get her family out of this poverty.

CHAPTER THIRTY-THREE

WHY TALENT DOES NOT TRANSLATE TO JOB?

-By Vishvajeet Patil

One day I went to buy a grill for my house. Just at the welding shop, one boy was working on welding. It was a really hot sunny day. He was sweating profusely. I went to him and asked, "Why don't you go inside and work?" He replied, "No, I am fine here". I thought of taking his interview for my Project, so I asked him if we could talk for some time. He hesitantly agreed.

We started interacting and he told me that his name was Mr. S and he was from U.P. His family still lived there. They had some land over there, where his father used to work. He also used to farm before he shifted to Pune. They used to grow crops according to the season.

He had been farming since a young age, as his economic condition was not very good. He was not educated, but from a young age, he was multi-talented. He was very good at different art forms. He wanted to be someone successful in his life. He always wanted to be self-reliant. So later, when he grew up, he came to Pune in search of a job and started working here in the welding shop. He said that he likes to work here because he knows about this stream the most.

However, he doesn't get enough money from his job. Before he joined this job as a fresher, he used to make lots of mistakes like using lightweight metal, not being able to complete before the deadline, etc and because of it, his boss used to cut his wages. Those days, he had to sleep hungry. Also most of the time, he needed to do overtime for money.

Later he told me that whenever he finds himself losing hope, he just calls his parents and after that, he feels calm and peaceful. His parents always gave him motivation and courage. He said, "Life is not easy, you always need to struggle and suffer through a lot of things to get something."

The only help he wants from the government is that there are lots of talented people in their stream, but they do not get the opportunity that they deserve. He wished that there should be an opening of jobs, not according to education, living, or status but according to talent.

In the end, he said,

"There are lots of people who have multiple talents, but not all of them are educated because of different-different reasons. It's completely understandable that education is important, but I think talent also matters the same!"

From his experience, I realized that if we have a high aim, I need to become a stubborn person to achieve it. Also, there are so many talented humans in our country but we are still providing jobs based on 10th, 12th, and graduate degrees. Yes, it is efficient to just screen-based on degrees but we should start screening based on their skills and talents in all the industries.

CHAPTER THIRTY-FOUR

LIFE OF A FAMILY MAN

-By Suhani Dwivedi

Interaction with Mr. P

The day I was given my English Project, I decided to interview an Uncle who sits near my society gate. Yes, correct our Watchman. He was on duty as a security guard when I went there and asked for permission to take his interview.

His name was Mr. P and he was 32 years old. He was from Jabalpur, Madhya Pradesh. He is married and has 2 kids. His family still lives in Jabalpur and his both children are studying in a private school over there. Only he had shifted to Pune to earn higher wages than he earns in Jabalpur. Also, he shared with me that he misses his wife, children, and parents a lot and doesn't like this watchman's job, but he is still doing it for his children. He does not want his children to drop out after 10th grade as he had to do because his family didn't have enough money for his higher education. He wants them to be more educated than him.

He has rented a home to live in Pune. He has food to eat every day but he doesn't get enough sleep due to his night shifts. He has suffered a lot in his life, mostly due to a shortage of money. His dream was to join the army, but he couldn't achieve that because of some family issues on top of monetary issues. He has been praying for his children, that they should have a decent and independent life.

One message that he wanted to give to society was,

"Education is more important than anything in our life. Without education we can't get a respected job, so be educated in your life and be independent."

In the end, I thought to ask, "What support do you want from the government?" He told me that the government should reduce inflation so that everyone could afford day-to-day commodities easily.

I learned from him that education is the most important thing in children's lives and that I should take it seriously if I want to fulfill my goals of being independent in the future.

CHAPTER THIRTY-FIVE

THE MAGIC & POWER OF MOTIVATION

-By Ganesh Kumbhar

Since we all have too many things to do, the best way to not feel hopeless is to get up and do something. We can't wait for good things to just happen to us. If we go out and make some good things happen, we could fill the world with hope, and also fill ourselves with hope.

I remember, when I was going to Keshav Nagar chowk, I saw a Vada pav vendor. I thought about talking with him for the interview, but I am not a talkative person. Still, I showed courage and went to him. I asked him, "Bhaiya, Are you comfortable sharing your life experience?" He replied that he was a little scared but asked me to visit him the next evening.

I went the next day and he started sharing. His name was Mr. G and he belongs to Pune. He was 27 years old and he has been selling Vada Pav for the last 6 years. He usually earns 200 to 600 rupees on daily basis.

When asked about his childhood, he shared that when he was young, his mothers and father died. He was in 6th or 7th grade and his younger brother Sushant was around 3-4 years old. He dropped out of school and started working in different houses to earn for himself and his brother. Later, he decided to enroll his brother in an orphanage for safety. As he grew up, he knew his strength and power. He realized that leaving education in between was the wrong decision in his life. He knew that education that aims at fostering students' positive values and attitudes is an essential element of a whole person. He wished he could have studied.

His dream was to be a bodybuilder in his life. He worked hard to provide his brother with an education by doing several jobs. Currently, he sells Vada pav and makes money from it. He has one aim - to fulfill his brother's needs and his all dreams. He wasn't able to make good enough money from selling Vada pav as people didn't come a lot to his stall. He was afraid and dejected. He thought if people won't come to his stall, then how would money for his brother's education come? Multiple ill thoughts used to come to his mind.

Then one of his friends encouraged and inspired him to grow and work harder towards his destination. He told,

> *"If people knew how hard I worked to achieve my mastery, it wouldn't seem so wonderful after all. Dreams can come true, but there is a secret. They're realized through the magic of persistence, determination, commitment, passion, practice, focus, and hard work."*

He worked harder in selling Vada pav and in a unique way his friend helped him in selling Vada pav. Some years later, his Vada pav became famous all around the Keshav Nagar. He believed in himself. Now he makes enough money to educate his brother.

I was inspired by his spirit to take care of his brother and learned that collaboration can take us a long way. He collaborated with his friend as a team. **Alone we can do so little, together we can do so much!**

Part 5: Tales of Endurance

CHAPTER THIRTY-SIX

A Life Without Struggles Is a Myth

-By Shraddha Singh

Interaction with Mr. V

When I was returning from school, it was raining heavily. I decided to wait on one side of the road for some time. There I discovered a small restaurant on the roadside. I waited near that restaurant, and while standing there, I started observing one Uncle who was operating everything there. I observed that even though it was raining heavily, he was on his task. I went to him. Before I could say anything, he asked me politely, "What do you want, Dear?". I asked him, "Uncle, will I get your precious time? I want to have a conversation about your life for one of my projects". Although he was working, he agreed to talk to me. Then we started with our conversation. His name was Mr. V and he was from Andhra Pradesh.

Uncle V told that he spent his childhood in Andhra Pradesh with his parents. He had 6 siblings. His parents were working as laborers to earn money and fulfill their family needs. He said that his father was quite strict as compared to his mother. At the age of 7, he started to go to school. He and his brothers were allowed to attend school but his sisters were not allowed. According to his father, girls doing household chores was more important than anything else. Then he taught his sisters some basic knowledge. His dream was to study till 10th grade but unfortunately, he failed in 7th grade and he was asked to drop out of school. He convinced his parents a lot to give him the second chance but they refused. At the age of 15, he started to work as a child laborer, and for 5 years, he did the same job keeping aside his big dreams.

At the age of 20, he got married. He decided to travel to Pune with his wife so that he could give a better life to his children. He came to Pune with 200 rupees and he told me that he didn't have any idea about what he would do here. Where would he live? What would he eat? He had no idea. At that time his relative gave him the job at his place, but he was not treating him properly even though he was working hard. His wage was too low. He tried to convince him to increase his wage, but he refused by saying, "You live with us, we pay for your household material. What more could you expect from us?"

After Uncle V's first child was born, his wife was suffering from blood deficiency and he didn't have enough money, so he donated his blood to someone, and then he arranged money to save his wife. He said that it was getting difficult for him to survive with less money and he was unable to fulfill his young daughter's dream. This used to make him feel that he is not a perfect father. After 3 years, the relative increased his wage as Uncle V's second child was born. His wife convinced him to start his restaurant as he was a good cook, but he refused and continued to work with the relative and he said that it was his biggest fault. After struggling a lot, he opened his fast food cart, which was a huge achievement for him. After working hard for one more year he closed his fast food cart and opened a small restaurant. Later, he also bought a small house.

During this pandemic, Coronavirus took his mother away. She was already suffering from Cancer, so Uncle V decided to go to Andhra Pradesh to visit her. He reached there but unfortunately, after some days his mother passed away. He was tortured by his brother a lot for all the property distribution but that is sorted and now he is happy with his small family. He sends his children to a good school. He said that his childhood destroyed his future, but he wants his children to have a better future. He is a successful person in his life.

I got a bit emotional when he shared his initial struggles of coming to Pune as my father had similar struggles. I would say that I got inspired by his story and one thing I learned is parents always work for their children and they have a very big role in building their children's life.

CHAPTER THIRTY-SEVEN

HOPES NEVER DIE

- By Anushka T. Mishra

Interaction with Mr. C

Big city, winter days, and the regular traffic. While I was traveling to my home I saw one Pani-puri vendor along with other vendors who were selling different things in a row at a chowk in Mundhwa, Pune. I was thinking, how do they survive? How many difficulties do they face in a day? Many more questions were coming to my mind. I decided to talk with them and I was eager to know about their life.

I chose one of the Pani-puri vendors whose name was Mr. C. He was from Jhansi, Uttar Pradesh. He was 29 years old. I started to go deep inside his life and he told me about his childhood. His childhood was decent and He used to live with his family. He used to go to school. He also shared that he is 10th pass.

Then he shared with me about his current situation. He had come here for work because he was married and he was living with his wife and they were not able to survive in Uttar Pradesh. He came to Pune with a lot of hopes but in this city also he was not getting a job. He started thinking, "Why did I come to Pune? My family will die. What should I do?" He was losing hope and all he was thinking of, was to go back to Uttar Pradesh. However, his wife told him that they could borrow money from someone and then start their own business as he could cook very nicely. She suggested, that he should start selling Pani-puri, Vada pav, or open a small hotel.

He started thinking about that and finally after struggling for 1 year, he decided to open a stall of Pani-puri. In the beginning, he faced many difficulties like people not eating his Pani-puri and sometimes they ate but they did not give him money. But this time, he did not lose his hope. He fought with that difficult time and now after 6 years, his life is quite better than before. His family can survive now. Now he has 2 cute children who are 2 and 3 years old.

When I asked him "What do you want from the government and people?". He said that he only wants one thing and that is the government officers should stop troubling them. They take their stall away and destroy it. They take money from them. And one thing that he wants from people is that when they are eating Pani-puri, they ensure to give money and not fight with him. He added,

"We are also human beings and we are doing hard work. If you don't want to give money, don't give but don't fight with us."

I got emotional while he shared his struggles. I learned that we should not lose our hope and if we have taken any work into our hands or have decided to do something, then we should finish it and not give up!

Also, we should keep learning new skills as it can help us anytime as cooking came handy to Mr. C.

CHAPTER THIRTY-EIGHT

HARD WORK CAN CHANGE LIFE

-By Aashitosh Gaud

I remember I was sitting with my mother when she shared with me a story of a man, which was quite inspirational, and that led me to interview him for my English Project. His name was Mr. G.

In childhood, he was poor. He didn't have his own home and also he didn't get food to eat two times a day. He had four brothers and his father used to work on a farm. The farm's owner was very inconsistent in providing salary on time. Mr. G was in a government school but he didn't have the proper resources to study. One day after the exam when the results came, his father saw that his child's marks were very low and then he asked him, "Why are your marks low?" Mr. G replied, "I don't have books to study". His father didn't reply anything and went to the owner for money. When he asked the owner for money, the owner replied, "I can't give you money, but if you want, then take my son's old book and give it to your children to study."

His father took those books with him and returned home. He gave those books to his children. With those books, Mr. G was able to score better marks in his 10th grade and he got a scholarship. With the scholarship money and some help from his brother's savings, he opened a tea stall with a big dream in his eyes but it did not survive long because it was a new shop and not many customers came to that stall.

He got depressed as all their savings got over. His brothers tried to help him out emotionally and financially. Then he started working in a milk dairy and saved some money. After a while, he again opened his tea stall with the help of his brothers, and leveraging the learnings from the last attempt, his tea stall gave a better result and in 6 years, he saved enough money to realize his dream of opening a small hotel and having a small house for his family.

When I asked Mr. G what he expected from the government, he said,

"I just want the Government to help every child to get a quality education."

From this experience, It struck me that my brain just stops working once I start feeling hungry then how could a child study if he/she does not get enough food to eat? It is indeed very hard or almost impossible to do.

Also, Mr. G inspired me to aim higher in life and learned that we should never lose our hope and work hard to strive for our aims. I was also able to resonate with a quote that says, '**Today's struggle is tomorrow's strength**'.

CHAPTER THIRTY-NINE

A SUCCESSFUL SHOPKEEPER

-By Nandini Giri

Interaction with Mr. D

Once our English Project surfaced, I had 2-3 people in mind whose story I could cover. One among them was the shopkeeper in my neighboring area. I stopped at his shop, asked for the chocolate, and kindly requested him for an interview on his life, he got a little confused and said, "I don't have time, I have many customers waiting". The next day I went to the same shop and requested him again for the interview with a bait. I said to him, "Uncle, your life story could be in a book and you could become famous". After listening to this, he quickly got interested and our conversation began.

His name was Mr. D, and he belonged to Gujarat. He had three brothers and he was the eldest. He wanted to do something big in his life but where they used to live, there were not many facilities available, so he came to Pune and started working as a helper in a shop and slowly he got information about how to run shops.

He opened his own shop with the help of his savings and family's help and started earning good money. In some years, he became more knowledgeable on how to do retail business. Later, he also started selling his products in the wholesale market and now he gets a decent amount of profit. Feeling accomplished in life, he wants to grow his wholesale business even more. When I asked him, "What help do you want from the government?" He replied, "I don't want more but I want the government to help everyone to do whatever they want to do."

I was inspired by his courage to leave his home state and come to Pune for accomplishing his dreams. I also got motivated by his growth from a helper to an owner and he continuously wants to grow. I will end the story with one quote from Oprah Winfrey which resonates with Uncle D life. He says,

"I've come to believe that each of us has a personal calling that is as unique as our fingerprint and the best way to succeed is to discover what you love and then find a way to offer it to others in the form of service and to do so, allow the energy of the universe to lead you."

CHAPTER FORTY

TOKEN OF HAPPINESS

-By Pooja Gupta

Interaction with Mr. H

Obstacles don't have to stop you. If you run into a wall, don't turn around and give up. Figure out how to climb it, go through it, or work around it. In life, every individual faces hard times at some point or another. It is those who never give up in such tough times that get to enjoy the fruits.

I met a person who is a cobbler. His name was Mr. H and he passes his days by singing and gossiping with his friends. He lives with his beautiful family. He was a person who had tough times and he wanted to give up everything. He knew that giving up would not make him triumph, so he showed courage and faced obstacles throughout his life.

I saw him while looking at the potential humans to interview. He was sitting and working on the footpath. I honestly felt sad after looking at his condition. I went nearby and talked to him softly. I requested him to tell me about his life journey and he began sharing.

His childhood was simple but painful. When he was around 9 to 10 years old, his parents passed away due to cancer. He had two sisters who were younger than him. He had to take responsibility. He was the only hope for his sisters. At an early age, he tried to make money. When he was a small kid, no one wanted to give him jobs but he never gave up. He used to do small-small things to make money. For example, by selling vegetables, flowers, toys, sometimes washing cars, and many other things. As a child, he did not understand the importance of education and struggled a lot because of it. When I asked him, "How important is education in your life?" He proudly told me,

> *"It helps people become better citizens, get a better-paid job, and shows the difference between good and bad. Education shows us the importance of hard work and, at the same time, helps us grow and develop. Thus, we are able to shape a better*

society to live in by knowing and respecting rights, laws, and regulations. "

I was blissful and glad to know that he knew the importance of education.

Later, when he grew up, he learned to read and write. He was passionate about doing things of his own and not under someone. So he thought of mending and polishing shoes all day long and thus earned his livelihood. However, it wasn't an easy job. He faced a plethora of negative judgments and demotivation. He was one of the courageous and fearless people who ignored all these comments, eventually continuing his work. People thought that he didn't make enough money by being a cobbler. Whoever has been thinking this is completely wrong. With this job, he was able to educate his sons and his children have grown up now and are earning on their own. One of his sons is the manager of a hotel and one of his sons is an engineer.

He has become older now, still, he is a cobbler because he loves being a cobbler. He doesn't feel ashamed about it, moreover, he is proud of it. He says that being emotionally dependent on other people can really make your life miserable. If that person fails to make you happy, you will become disappointed and frustrated. Happiness from others is not very reliable. So, if you are capable enough then do what makes you happy even if you become older.

When you choose to do what makes you happy, you instantly build your confidence. You are telling yourself that you are worthy and deserving of soaking up every bit of happiness that you can! When you choose to do what makes you happy, you will have no room to sink into your insecurities because happiness triumphs over them.

This interaction just made my day and gave me learnings about being emotionally and financially independent. It taught me to accept the harsh realities of life, find happiness in tiny things and keep exploring things that could provide my token of happiness in life.

Afterword

Who sells garbage bags, who sells tea,
Who sells toys, who clean the roads for thee,
All of them are part of me,
My unseen side, no one is ready to see.
I am here as the village is empty for me,
The developed Pune was a ray of hope for me.
It's the feeling of a small fish in a shark's sea,
As my unseen side, no one is ready to see.
Some call me a thief, some call me lazy,
I have an Identity, are you crazy?
My child's future is definitely hazy,
My unseen side is not at all glazy.
Every day I sweat like a watering tap,
But seldom finds happiness on my map.
Right to equality sound funny to me,
As my unseen side, no one is ready to see.
What will I ask the government to meet?
They call us the 'stigma of the developed street'.
Even the sun rises with darkness for me,
As my unseen side, no one is ready to see.
Problem rains cats and dogs on me,
But my family holds their feet for me,
They are the only hope which rebuilds me,
As my unseen side, no one is ready to see.
I'm waiting for ages to be a part of the sea,
But I don't know when this sea would let me be.
Sometimes I feel, I'm not a human bee,
As my unseen side, no one is ready to see.

-**Empathetic Humans** (*July 2022*)